On Why the Quiltmaker Became a Dragon

On Why the Quiltmaker Became a Dragon

A Visionary Poem

by Sheila Nickerson

Illustrations by Judy Cooper

Published by Vanessapress
© 1985

The Editorial Board of Vanessapress wishes to thank the following for their assistance in this publication: to Eva Bee and Donita Haynes for typesetting and layout; to Larry Laraby for his supportive advice and generosity; to Sheila Nickerson for her cooperative nature and kindness of spirit; and to all the wonderful folks who contributed their hard earned bucks towards the production of this project. And, finally, to Pat Monaghan who got us all into this publishing business in the first place, we extend a very dubious thank you.

Book Design by Jan Sanders Leone and Spirit Mountain Press
Typeface is Zapf

Typeset by Spirit Mountain Press
Printed by MacNaughton & Gunn

FIRST EDITION
ISBN: 0-914221-04-3

Introduction

Wind rapping rudely at the window, rattling knuckles sharply. A woodstove tightly straining against the cold. Quilt across your knees, as much to keep you company as to keep out the cold. Everyone else in the house in bed, asleep, snoring lightly, unaware that you are sleepless, restless, eyes moving in a lonely vigil from window to door to book and back to window. It is the darkest hour of night, the time when things of the world and things of the imagination become confused and blend. Priorities become reversed, reality becomes less orderly, more fanciful. Here you are neither wife nor mother nor lover nor friend; you are merely woman. Who are you really? From what substance are you formed?

You pull the quilt closer about you to ward away the chill. Patterns of the past dance before you, stitched images long forgotten resurrect themselves in form and color and substance. There is the girl child who could beat up any boy in the fifth grade. There is someone named Sarah who carries in her head unspeakable knowledge but silently takes her daughter to a movie. There is the violent image of a dead woman, her body emptied of a child and frozen. There is the picture of many women circled around a quilt frame, needles flashing, heads bent, mouths bristling with pins. Who are they? They're only dreams, fantasies, illusions, night dancers of the mind. They have no substance, no meaning. Do they?

Think, if you will, of a woman in a small Alaskan town who agrees to help quilt the stories of the town's past. There are stories that are pleasant and some that are frightening but need to be told. There are stories filled with power. As the woman quilts something happens to her vision. Things in her mind's eye become more real, more pressing, more demanding than the "real" things around her. She soars in what could be imagination; reality takes on new color and shape.

Of course, it's only a poem. Isn't it?

— BJ Webb
Editorial Board
Vanessapress

"...she stitched her story on black/silk patches from the mourning dress, quaint/as our novels will seem...."
                    — Mei-mei Berssenbrugge

Variable Star #1

I woke one morning
under goosedown--tired of poems,
tired of pushing words
while others rake, hoe, sew.

I buried those words:
a village of children
dead of influenza.
Their vague names
will soon be lost.

Now I fall down
before bathtubs and flowerbeds,
kneel on Tibetan carpets,
hold up in my hands
potatoes and wild mint--
the real prayer.

I chant calico, velvet,
place lace on the mountains,
make broken landscapes whole
with cloth, stone, needle, skin.

Wild Goose Chase. Variable Star.
Swing in the Center.
Catch Me if You Can:

Once quilt-maker, I now unravel patterns.
Thread, color, pictures:
These I now give back
in order to take back
all I gave away.

9

Road to California

Power, I have learned,
comes not from holding down
but letting go.

Wind blows in geraniums
here on the coast of Mexico,
where I have come, a visitor.
Small birds fly through palms.
All can be divined
in the heart of the lobster
while I, frog-mountain woman
from the north, from Alaska,
must find my slow way back,
creature of dead reckoning.
Ruby-throated hummingbirds
in rain-wet geraniums,
let me tell you my tale.

> *Ship's Wheel. Straight Furrow.*
> *Road to California:*

Unrolling the spool of time,
we came to the bicentennial of America,
the time to celebrate, record,
collect the pictures of our years.
We, the women, were asked
to quilt that history down.
You know how it goes--
the visions we are meant to have,
the primitive simplicity
of how and where we live;
it is expected.

Birds in the Air #1

Wild Goose Chase and Variable Star.
Mariner's Compass. House in the Country:

We got the visions down.

Birds in the Air
and Old Maid's Puzzle.
Tree Everlasting. Path of Thorns:

We got the visions down:
Black Velvet Raven, Discovery of Gold,
Alpenglow.
Log Cabin Church, Raven Block Print,
Old Courthouse.

Holy Trinity Church, Red Dog Saloon,
Skunk Cabbage.

Five squares across, seven down:
thirty-five states on a field
of orange and black.

Box and Star. Tumbling Blocks.
Delectable Mountains:

I remember the Tailor of Gloucester.
I remember Joseph and his coat of many colors.
I remember...
I used to be a sewing woman.

Then, we came to the centennial of my town
(let it have any name).
This time, I was not asked to quilt

11

Hovering Hawk

but knew I was stuck at the quilting table.
Across the street from Centennial Hall
which we built on West Third Street:

"Sweet Violet's Virtue
Custom Sewing with
Imagination"

The sign hangs in a window
with stained glass visions--
wheat, lupine, a parrot.
Outside, against gray boards,
a bicycle waits, metal escape.
The battered door stays blue and shut.
(You need to know, if you dye with lupine,
it turns cloth to a bitter green.)

Secret Drawer. Orange Peel.
Horn of Plenty:

Once, I was recording.
Now, I am making.
Once, I was repairing.
Now, I am creating.

Sweet Violet, take me into
your fingertips,
your needle's sweet seeking.
Hem me with lupine and feathers
into the boards of your house,
into the numbers of your address,
into the alphabet of color.
Let me stay for a while

12

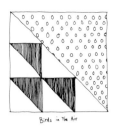
Birds in The Air

in your weathered house
where all can be repaired,
made new, dyed green
like the bitter blood of April.

> *Birds in the Air*
> *and Old Maid's Puzzle.*
> *Baby Blocks and Tree Everlasting:*

Still I will fly from you
like a magic spool
over mountaintops.

Colonial women boasted
of the number of spools
they spent per quilt.
Not I.
Southern women preferred
white and pink.
Not I.
I will go make rain.
I will take bliss
in the melting of myself.
Then, Sweet Violet,
like a spider I will float
to you down mountain mists.
I will wind myself in your hair,
nest in your Imagination,
lay eggs in your basket of scraps.

> *Eccentric Star and Mariner's Compass,*
> *Star of Bethlehem and Joseph's Coat:*

Melon Patch

How will I explain these changes?
How will I explain
what I do up there on mountaintops,
making the moisture of life,
winding my body at will?
What will I say to the women
still following the needle,
still pouring their lives
through the eye of a needle?

Ships at Sea. Birds in the Trees.
Circles and Crosses. Basket of Scraps.
Schoolhouse. Straight Furrow.
Job's Tears:

No Colonial woman, no quilt-making woman
sewing over the frame of gossip
ever before became a dragon
taking the shape of the clouds.

Sunshine and Shadow,
Streak of Lightning.
Melon Patch and Ocean Waves:

Some got up and left the quilting table,
but none became a serpent.

Fly Foot. Field of Diamonds.
Rainbow. Sailboat. Bars:

I am the cloud you see
falling, rising.

14

Catch Me If You Can

Fannie's Fan and Harvest Sun.
Steps to the Altar.
Eye of God:

I am the cloud you see
falling, rising.

Attic Window. Crazy.
Trip Around the World.
Rocky Mountain Road:

You do not know my rhythm.
I am the song of the crocus,
the soul of the toad
sleeping in winter mud.
I am the mother of darkness
rising out of mountain ponds.
In case you did not know it,
night comes from earth, not sky.
The origin of night has not been found.

You see me stitching my days together
but do not see me.
You see me as mother, wife,
keeper of houses and time;
but you do not see.
You do not understand
the ways of dragons
and mud maidens,
the way I see
through the roots of sleeping things.

15

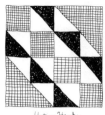
Hovering Hawks

Amethyst, ermine, ruby:
I carry talismans
more powerful than light.
You see me holding socks,
pants, plates--Blue Onion,
Viceroy--that is only
the crack in your eye.
I live beyond your field of vision,
go in and out doors of red and blue,
disappear in rain,
roll in the ecstasy of what is wet.

Mother of worms and streams,
this is my song:

    Mud, root, spruce,
    beach, coast, cloud,
    skunk cabbage and slug,
    soul of whale and soul of shell,
    climb the ladder of rain.

I am the top.
I am the roof of the rain.

Break the jade screen.
You will see me there
on bridge, river bank, cloud.
Wearing moss, eating lichen,
holding to a shape like smoke,
I will greet you with
the cold, wet kiss of life.

16

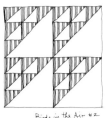
Birds in the Air #2

The oceans of your body,
the tides of your heart
come to me, return from me.

I speak through the voice of rain
to the timpani of ravens.
I know the language of gutters,
rainspouts, creeks in spring;
I can crash through glass
or land without being known.

Steeplechase.
Birds in the Air.
Catch Me if You Can.
Rocky Road to Kansas.

I carry the record of exploration.
Sir Francis Drake came out
of my imagination.
Magellan sails my mind.
What Sweet Violet sews
is nothing by comparison.
Cook, La Perouse, Malaspina--
those who found Alaska's coast--
ride in my bloodstreams forever.
Those who gave themselves to shipwreck,
who entered the brokenness of shells,
sleep in my lullaby of mist.
I can recall them at will,
recite their names like a chant,
sing the words of their logs.
Just listen to the ships
that foundered in Alaska:

17

Ocean Waves

SOPHIA, THREE SAINTS, CLARA NEVADA
ELNA, CROWN REEFER, CATHERINE SUDDEN
EDITH, SADIE, JOHN P. GAINES
DAWSON CITY, DORA
PRINCE GEORGE and PRINCESS KATHLEEN
PRINSENDAM

Crazy. Cube. Eccentric Star.
Flying Geese. Grandma's Dream:

I was out there in the foundering
but I never quilted these--
the shipwrecks grinding rocks
to glass, the lives that floated
out from coffin holds,
the broken toys that found their way
to frozen, oiled beaches
along with suffocated porpoises.

Log Cabin. Gothic Windows.
Nine-Patch Block.
Ocean Waves and Old Maid's Puzzle:

Never have we quilted
shipwreck, disease, prison,
the story of the daughter
who ran away from home,
the failures necessary as rain,
the lessons dark as ravens.

18

Old Maid's Puzzle

Finally, throwing down the quilt,
I collected all the broken lives
I kept like scraps in a basket,
rose up again in cloud,
danced on mountaintops
until I burst,
came down with sounds of shells,
ceremonial rattles, and grouse
crying for mates in the springtime woods
(hooters). You have heard.
Already you have heard.
What do I say?

> Grouse and shell,
> spruce and rock,
> blood and salt,
> berry and bone,
> I carry you all
> in my waterfall love.
> I dance for you all
> in the storm of my love.
> I gather you all
> in the rain of my love.
> You are the words.
> I am the notes;
> The coast,
> the orchestra I conduct.

In March when color creeps
quietly into the woods,
it carries my blood.
How else could the blueberry
blossoms find their pink

19

Wild Goose Chase

in the dark of the winter woods?
And where does the juice
of the berry start?
Where does color begin?

We think of a crab as bloodless,
but it isn't.
Its heart is as real as a rabbit's.
Its blood is blue with iodine.
Deep in, our blood is blue.

Color begins with the rain.
I generate the color of rain,
I who seemed to be a cloud.
Sound begins with the rain.
Listen to timber in spring.

Fish fly out from the mouth of the spruce,
flowers from the eye of the fish,
trees from the ears of the totems--
from Whale, Dog Shark, Raven.

With its magical eyes
the halibut can see
what no one else can see,
and its cousin, starry flounder,
can bloom in any water,
fresh or salt.
Out of soapstone,
out of jade, out of flesh
it is the same.

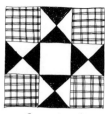

Variable Star #2

After rain, the woods
still smell of fish.
You have noticed. You know you have.
But you thought it was your imagination.
And you have noticed shapes in clouds,
a presence in the fog.
You have heard of Southeast Woman
and of Skagua, the Wind.

> *Field of Diamonds. Double Square.*
> *Barn Raising. Rocky Mountain Road:*

Why is it, when you walk
in woods, you know
you're not alone?

To keep making blood
that is colorless--
to keep filling streams and oceans,
to keep taking back
the essence of all that's born,
to keep pushing it out
through the needle of spring
with the thimble of eye:
My work is endless as rain,
the beginning of rain.

> *Circling Swallows.*
> *Wild Goose Chase. Variable Star.*
> *Catch Me if You Can:*

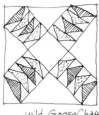
wild Goose Chase

Once I was known as a goddess
before the official religions
shrank me, made me shadowy
as the mists I inhabit,
made me gossamer and fey.
They tried to make me
a substitute
for lost concubines.
But wells and springs never forget
and those who read feng-shui
and hold the dowsing rod with faith.

> *Peace and Plenty.*
> *Wild Goose Chase.   Variable Star:*

Look to the bend in the river.

Sometimes a poet remembers me--
how I repaired the sky,
how I created out of mud,
how I made love with waters.
Oracle of gutters,
I grow you messages of grass
waving along your roof.
Grackles peck at my seeds.
Ravens delight in me.
If only you would look
to grass on your roof,
you would know.

> *Flower Pot. Drunkard's Path.*
> *Geometric Star:*

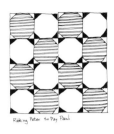
Robbing Peter to Pay Paul

I was born again,
a woman of the Second World War.
I was sewing, blocking, repairing buttons and hems,
taking my place
at the table of scraps.

All that time, I could have been
making a poem,
taking the rills of the mountainsides,
turning them into words,
taking the mist of the morning,
turning it into a book.
But I had to make a thousand squares
for other people's quilts
before I saw.

> *Diamond. Bars. Lost Ship.*
> *Robbing Peter to Pay Paul:*

Now the dragon turning, turning.
I drop these scales, each
a picture quaint as a Tiffany window--
Oyster Bay framed by wisteria.
Here, a bird; there, a jewel.
Here, a kiss that caused
the house to sway,
the world to roll
with fault lines through the stars.
The dragon flashes back in mist.
Was it there at all?
Maybe it was sun
glinting off the needles
of our woman hands,

23

Ocean Waves

our woman quilt,
the black and orange
checkerboard of days.

I am confluence.
When you enter my body,
you enter the waters of the world,
the flow of the stars.
I am clothed with flowers and mist.
Petals hang from my gauze-white dress,
but I am not gauze.
My feet are trees and rocks.
I have been consort, goddess, girl.
My colors are green and blue
with rainbow spots.
My eyebrows are reeds.
Am I ghostly or real?
Do you feel the rain
on your face?
Have you felt yourself grow strong?

Pinwheel.   Pineapple.
Triangle.   Prickly Path:

From quilt-maker to dragon lady,
from cloth to cloud,
from copying to creating,
from a single bed
to the world as a bed.
I give you mist,
you give me shape.
We belong.

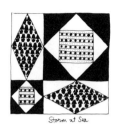

Storm at Sea

Fence Posts. Log Cabin.
Schoolhouse. Ship's Wheel.
Catch Me if You Can:

I live in a space like light.
Blueberries blossom here,
chyrsanthemums. I pull wool
over the scales,
forget permutation,
set tables with antique forks,
blow dust from the back of shelves,
teach the multiplication tables
as if all depended on numbers,
as if all were not
zero in zero,
a bright bubble blown
from the gorge of beginnings.
My robes are evanescent
as a rainbow in spring.
They flow with desire.
They flutter with petals,
even here on the hard north coast
where color hides,
where lilacs hardly dare.

Feathered Star. Princess Feather.
Indian Chintz. Gothic Windows.

Centennial, centennial:
What are one hundred years
but a hundred appliques?
How many stitches does one year take?
How many spools of thread?

25

Churn Dash #1

How many times must the needle
go in and out, up and down?
What does it take to anchor
ravens in flight?

If I were to cut a square
to place on the quilt today,
it would melt in my hands,
burst at the touch of a needle,
then rise like a mist
over the bent heads
of the women at work,
find its way out the window
like a soul released from bone.
Have you noticed how smoke, or mist,
floating over a town
delights in itself?

> *Broken Dishes. Broad Arrow.*
> *Noon and Night and*
> *Road to Tennessee:*

I see a vision--this woman
of mist and flowers
rising from a stream.
She's made of cloud
but strong enough
to take you in her arms.
She gives you the light
of vision. You give her shape.
Small flowers cling to her folds.
She holds the pink of spring
within her, hidden.

26

Broken Dishes

Winged Square. Star and Chain.
Hole in the Barn Door.
Triple Irish Chain:

I am the voice of the moss.
You can hear the chords
of the pushing buds,
the swelling pink
stronger than dark.

Unnamed, I name everything.
I grow into an entity of clouds.

Village Green. Lover's Knot.
Twin Sisters. Broken Dishes:

I bore children,
then ran from them up hillsides,
hiding in clouds
till the danger had passed.
Now they come to me on my terms.
I left the house full of toys,
the wearisome plates
and the hungry mouths
all opening and shutting like clams.

Where I live is no place for children.
I walk with flowers and mist,
am never cold,
can take any shape,
can hold any human form.

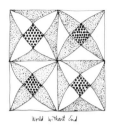

World Without End

I see the woman I have become
tall as the oldest spruce,
strong as waterfalls in spring,
delicate as mist.

What is the echo of my song?
I have no echo,
only the original.

Draconian, I gird the mountain stream.

> *Honeycomb and Hexagon Star.*
> *Churn Dash. Jacob's Ladder.*
> *Jack-in-the-box. Indian Hatchet.*
> *Catch Me if You Can:*

This is the vision of the quilt-maker
rising from the table of cloth:
The flat, square pictures fall
to the floor like an outworn skin.
Reptilian, transcendent, I arise.
With wings, scales, and tail
I burst through windows
past gardens, fences,
the patchwork neighborhood
I have sewed together all these years
and offered as the history of my time.
O remember Ruth and Anne and Grace and
Liz and Caroline and Betsy, Judy, Mary,
Mia, Carol, Betty, Jane, and Margaret.
Remember all the stitches,
borders and batting,
the albums, autographs and applique,

28

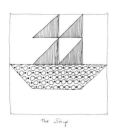
the Ship

the baskets and the cakes,
the children shared and yards filled up
with running through the crocuses,
with sunshine and shadow.

Snowflower. Kaleidoscope.
Hands All Around:

In the woods I find relief.
Where streams climb down
dark mountainsides I find
my way. Snails, worms, frogs
attend. Fish leap in the pools
cleared by the floods of spring.
Rainbows drink from the roots
of spruce and alder. Rocks
rejoice with the dance of moss.
As I breathe fire of creation,
lovers turn in their beds,
reach out from their sheeted flesh
to touch the sense of light
that ripples through their quilts.
A dawn breaks over the village,
this place I have known by many names,
this place I have sewed together
square upon square, careful colors
matched, while all the time my heart
was bursting to be born.
Come lap the drinkable light
from the stream I now command.
It will fill your mind
with lilies till it breaks
then take you where I am.

29

Road to California

The armor of my scales will fade.
Your arms and legs will grow
as strong as trees.
You will know that a thousand years
have passed, that what were once
dark spaces in the sky
have filled with stars.
Astronomers read the changing pattern
of variable stars
but still do not know distance.
Each day, the Crab Nebula
grows in diameter
by more than 100 million miles.

Barn Raising and Lover's Knot.
Maple Leaf and Whirligig.
Road to California:

The ontology of dragons
now takes the place of stitches
and embroidery.
All becomes more clear in rain.
Raven. Raven.
Song of meadows and of whales.
Today I found myself.

Let me start a new chapter,
a new view of the vision.
It begins like this:
I was a woman, invited and expected
to sew. Someone was retiring,
or having a baby.
I brought my patch of picture

30

Variable Star #2

to the quilt. My square was velvet
mountains under moonlight,
with strips of rickrack lace for snow.
I commemorated history.
I recorded what I knew,
what was expected.
I celebrated expectation
with scissors and design.

At the quilting table,
my view was stretched and framed,
joined to other views,
stitched to other women's windows.
Then, it was done—
the town we called our own,
the place we made again each day,
each time we looked into our yards
and anchored them with thread--
against the wind,
against time,
against the strange omen
of three ravens arriving at once.

> *Hole in the Barn Door.*
> *Wild Goose Chase and Variable Star.*
> *Checkerboard. Sawtooth. Save All:*

Sisters of thread,
I leave you here,
inviting you to follow
up where flowers truly bloom
in calico beneath the snow,

31

Rocking Peter to Play Piano

up where flowers grow
forever in my rainbow hold,
no cold, no cold at all.

Diamond in the Square.
Diagonal Triangles.
Geometric Star:

I cut it from my eyes and heart,
offered it there on the table.
No one ate it.
All sewed silently
while the words in my heart
went in and out like this:

Dye of lupine
eye of forget-me-not
brain of boat and church
honor of skunk cabbage
integrity of meadow
I lie down in you all
roll in your color
I know you and the women
who made you
their stories
a window frozen in cloth.

Carpenter's Wheel. Eccentric Star.
Seek-no-further.
Catch Me if You Can:

32

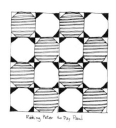
Robbing Peter to Pay Paul

One day I walked inside
the quilt we made. This is what happened:
I am in a meadow,
mountains not too far away,
flowers at hand.
A magical raven
brings me a message
in a lupine seed, a song:
There is a town of gold,
but not where you expect.
Follow deeper, into the meadow's heart.
Ask dandelions where to go.
Ask dandelions. Ask alpenglow.
Ask dandelions where to go.

Double Wedding Ring. Box and Star.
Kansas Sunflower:

Then I read in the paper
about the frozen family
found in a snow-covered hut
near Barrow, dead since 1510.
The 42-year-old woman had recently
delivered a baby, missing,
probably buried in a tunnel to the hut.
There was a young woman, too,
in her twenties. Both had black lungs.
According to Dr. Zimmerman, they suffered
from parasitic worms and osteoporosis,
a softening of the bones
caused by lack of sunlight.

33

Ocean Waves

Flying Geese. Field of Diamonds.
Grandma's Dream. Spider Web:

Let me tell (for we will not quilt)
the story of the S.S. Princess Sophia.
She left Skagway for Seattle
on the night of October 23, 1918,
with 343 men, women, and children.
Her hold kept horses and gold,
a summer's haul from the Yukon and beyond,
and Christmas parcels for soldiers in France.
She was the last ship out before winter,
glory and celebration,
bright lights on the dark way south.
At 2:00 a.m., in a blizzard,
she struck Vanderbilt Reef,
40 miles north of Juneau in Lynn Canal.
She foundered for two days while Captain Locke
refused aid. A sister ship, **Princess Alice,**
was on her way from Vancouver.
There was no immediate danger.
Standing by was a chain of ships
like a song:
U.S. lighthouse tender **Cedar,**
U.S.S. Peterson, King & Winge
Estabeth, Anita Phillips,
Amy, Excursion, Elinor,
Elsinore, Lone Fisherman.
In the first dark
of October 25, in raging snow,
Sophia *rolled off the reef and sank.*
No one survived. No one. But they didn't
drown. They died of exposure, or suffocated
in oil, along with porpoises and murres.
The final conversation with **Sophia**
went like this:
Sophia: *"Taking water and foundering.*

Catch Me If You Can

For God's sake come and save us."
Cedar: "Coming full speed but cannot see
on account of thick snows and taking heavy seas."
Sophia: "All right, but for God's sake hurry.
Water coming in the room." Soon after:
"Just time to say goodbye. We are foundering."

When the frozen bodies from the Sophia
were stacked on the Juneau docks in October 1918,
in the days of influenza,
the town lacked enough caskets.
The Masonic funeral of
John F. Pugh, Customs Collector
for Alaska, had to be held in private
because of the epidemic.
And during that time, it is said,
the prostitutes turned nurse.
During that time, much was said.

The Alaska Daily Empire read:
Saturday, October 26, 1918:

PRINCESS SOPHIA SINKS AND
350 SOULS PROBABLY PERISH
"This disaster wipes out
many of the best people of the Interior,"
said J. C. Rathbone.

Monday, October 28, 1918:
158 OF PRINCESS SOPHIA'S DEAD RECOVERED;
ALL HOPE THAT ANY SURVIVE IS ABANDONED

The diary of passenger John Maskell
was found. It said, "We are surrounded
by a number of small boats, but it is

35

the Ship

too rough to transfer. Realizing
that we are surrounded by grave danger,
I make this my last will."

It was reported: "One woman was found
who had several thousand dollars in diamonds.
The watch of A.W. Kendall, one of the victims,
stopped at six o'clock. Several of the watches
had stopped at between six and seven o'clock."

In the Alaska Daily Empire
it was reported:
"Walter J. O'Brien, agent
for the Canadian Pacific at Dawson,
who with his wife and five children
were (sic) lost on the Princess Sophia,
was clasping his son closely
in his arms when his body was found.
Difficulty was experienced
in releasing the child."

Playing at the Palace was The Pugilist
with Charlie Chaplin and Fatty Arbuckle.

It was said that some of the bodies
carried considerable sums in Liberty Bonds,
War Savings Stamps, Bank Drafts, and currency.

By November 5, the reports had dwindled.
Divers recovered the body of Charles A. Paddock
and a safe with $62,000 worth of gold.
Diver Thomas Veitch found the body
of a horse near the safe.
The ship was broken in two,
the staterooms swept clean
by currents.

Birds in the Air #2

Walter Harper and his bride,
Episcopal missionaries from Ft. Yukon
bound for war work,
were buried together in Juneau;
he had been with the first party
to climb Mt. McKinley.
The Harpers' quilt is green and white,
embroidered with hundreds of names.

On the night of November 11, 1918,
in the dark of Armistice Day,
Princess Alice brought
156 bodies into Vancouver.
The Great War was over.

The English setter found at Tee Harbor,
only living thing to survive
(and which we talk about more
than the seventeen frozen children),
went to live with the miners
at Last Chance Basin, safely
out of the reach of the sea.

Only one letter survives from the wreck.
Private Auris W. McQueen, Signal Corps,
to "Dear Mama":
"The decks are all icy,
and this wreck has all the marks
of a movie stage setting.
All we lack is the hero and the vampire.
I am going to quit, and see if I can rustle
a bucket and a line to get some sea water
to wash in. We are mighty lucky
we were not all buried in the sea water."

Old Maid's Puzzle

There are only some packets
of personal effects,
escheated property,
left in the State Museum.
I have held them: rusted eyeglasses,
keys to mysterious doors,
tokens and trinkets,
naturalization papers and visas,
tickets for the ride to death.
And some were children's.
George Allen was a Turk,
Carl Knutson was a Swede.

What if I made a song
of the names of the dead?
Ableson, Bourne, and Brown.
Castleman, Cousins, and Eade.
Ironside, Kendall, and Kirk.
McDonald, O'Brien, and Ryan.
Sutherland, Walker, and Wright.

What if I made up a diary
from this time of disaster
and told you it came from the hand
of Miss Eleanore Very, a passenger?
She lived, I might tell you,
in Green Valley, Indiana,
a farmer's daughter
adept at piano and lace.
She had gone to Dawson City
to visit her twin sister Susannah

38

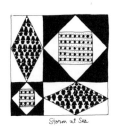
Storm at Sea

who had married a clergyman of the Methodist faith
and was giving birth in the wild.
The child and sister had died.
She was returning to Indiana
to meet her fiance returning from France.
As soon as the war was over,
they would marry, settle down
in the house of an ancient aunt
on Maple Street, across from
the Courthouse in Green Valley,
just up the street from the schoolhouse.
For them there would be
no rocky road to California,
only the shade of the Tree of Life
in the town square in Green Valley.

What are my sources, you ask?
None but imagination.
How can you believe anything I say?
You can't.
(The Hitler diaries, remember,
were a swindle, and many others beside.)

> *Pineapple. Pandora's Box.*
> *Yankee Puzzle. Crazy.*
> *Rocky Road to Kansas.*
> *Catch Me if You Can:*

You see why I couldn't stay:
No one wanted (especially the men)
cemeteries, foundered ships, sickness,
prison, deserted children
frozen in cloth

39

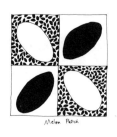

Melon Patch

for visitors to see
when they came
to Centennial Hall.
I had no choice.
I had to leave.
Miraculously (and this is news:
miracles aren't really miracles
but a sudden coming awake),
I could take the shape I chose,
and what I chose was a dragon shape,
for the dragon, made of cloud,
is life itself.

Attic Windows.   Gothic Windows.
Grandmother's Flower Garden.
Starry Path:

At dawn, a bird sings
the seam of my mountain back,
and I stir, turning the green
of the forest,
turning the dark of the tide.
Dew shakes from the trees.
Birds remember to push.
My eyes open like caves.
Down in the village I left,
daffodils turn. Children chirp.
The yards fill up
with sunshine and shadow.
Women take up their cloth
under the Tree Everlasting,
lance the light with needles,
border the day with silk.

Birds in The Air

Kaleidoscope, Prickly Path.
Lady in the Lake:

When you see morning mist
hanging in air
like a memory of night,
I am there.
Like the great sea turtle
of the southern reefs
I have dropped my eggs--
amethyst and jade--
and waded back to my place.
They will hatch and make
their way after me,
many snatched by birds
of brilliant beak and eye
and carried to nests
of dark desire.

American Indians thought
all that was
rested on the back of a turtle.

I will generate new eggs.
I will guard them in my body
till the time is right.
I will plant them like bulbs.
My children are crocuses
with a core of precious stone.
No matter how you snatch them,
they come back; they come back.
Unlike pictures on quilts,
they come back,

41

Variable Star #1

bearing the blood of my moisture.
If you stop by a mountain stream,
if you look into a muskeg pool
where night begins,
you will see.
But please be advised,
I am very fond of swallows.
If you have dined on swallows,
I will catch you
as you cross my stream.

House in the Country. Rainbow.
Straight Furrow. Bow Tie:

I am the woman who
finds new ways
to tell my story.
You can, too,
if you dare walk in
to the quilt you have made.

I take my scales off
like a pillowcase,
replace them with skin,
silk, chintz, chenille,
chamois, and crepe de Chine.
I deal with rickrack and lace,
eyelets and hooks,
undoing each day
the dress of my life.

Wild Goose Chase

Each day I stand before you
different. Only the color
of my eye remains the same.
As you look at me,
I change.

I am dragon and woman,
mist and earth,
sorrow and joy,
a dance of negative ions.
I carry colors
more poignant than birth.
When you enter my body,
you enter the matrix of stars.
You become a sun-grazing comet.
The astronomer Heinrich Kreutz
would have studied you,
numbered you.
Already, a Department of Defense
satellite named the P78-1
is chasing you.
Your heart is rock and ice
which bursts, then streams
behind you like a tail.
When you touch my hidden eggs,
you shake with their power.
You know the grace of amethyst,
the creation of crystal.

You think it is a question
of taking off clothes,
like stripping mica from a rock.
No, it is more than nakedness.

43

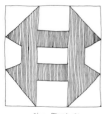
Churn Dash #1

It is permutation.
It is the eating of rainbows,
the drinking of light,
the swallowing of lilies,
the love of opposite things.
Refraction, reflection, dispersion.
Come sit at my table of rainbows.
Come eat from my plate of rain.
Admire the pattern
that cannot be repeated,
the pattern of variable stars,
novas exploding.

How are dragons different from rainbows?
How are daffodils related to rocks?
How is history different from grass?
Drink from the stream of light
and you will know.
All riddles ride in my blood.

Now, I must remember my songs.
What does a dragon woman say?

Snail and mouse and blueberry bush
porcupine, loon and toad
dragonfly, seal, and mink,
killer whale
seashell and petal and wind
Take my scales
and give me your skin
Let me remake the world
Let me undress and

Birds in the Air #1

let me unravel
Let me remake the world
Halibut, ptarmigan, deer
hummingbird, squirrel, and owl
humpback whale
bring me your voices
let me come out
more shapely than clouds
Let me marry you all
with wreaths of crocuses
bracelets of pearls
Let me remake the world.

Rejoice in the rain--
how I touch you--
how I smooth your skin with wind,
how I sing in the storm
that surrounds you.
Rejoice in your skin,
whether scale, granite, or wet.
Rejoice in touch,
which can come
in many ways.

From caves of quilt and stone
I come, carrying feathers,
flowers, and patterns
of fern and shell,
pebble and star.
My imprint is everywhere,
even the ellipse of your orbit,
the dive you take
into my corona,

Road to California

the images burned into you.
I know, you think you need
only take your singed clothes
to Sweet Violet's Virtue
on West Third Street
in the shadow of Centennial Hall
and be repaired.

O mortal, you are wrong.
There is no repair but deeper burning,
no place of mending
but in the corona
of my dragon heart.

Remember, the solar radius is 430,000 miles,
and the solar corona reaches millions of miles
into space, and the universe is expanding.
I am more than a star.
I will keep you with me
orbiting through every spring and fall,
the equinox and solstice of my eye.
Astronomers will sand their glasses finer
to follow all you sun-grazers,
numbering you,
placing you in large, black books,
until your hearts of rock and ice
have burst, streaming out behind you,
visible.

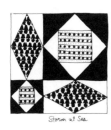
Storm at Sea

Every time you turn to Sweet Violet
and her lacquered box of thread,
I will heave,
undulating mountainsides
like northern lights.
No one will know the reason,
expecting only earthquakes.

> *Storm at Sea and Spider Web.*
> *Stripes and Trip Around the World.*
> *World Without End:*

Leave the fitting room.
Leave the scraps and shreds
and gather up
the clothes of air.

There is only time to say goodbye.

Consider the ravens: for they
neither sow nor reap...and
God feedeth them....
Consider the lilies how they grow:
they toil not, they spin not:
and yet I say unto you,
that Solomon in all his glory
was not arrayed like one of these.
And according to Tlingit mythology,
God Raven was white in the beginning;
Raven was the beginning.

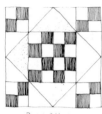
Road to California

"His Eye is on the Sparrow."
I have heard that
in the coldest places on the earth,
even the Quaker church in Kotzebue,
and know it to be true,
even the dock where the frozen bodies
from the *Sophia* were stacked like wood,
coffinless, and in the buried hut
outside of Barrow, and in the lost
passageways where baby bones are kept,
and on the floor of Lynn Canal
where horse bones lie
with harnesses and spoons,
and in our yards where all
out autumn leaves fall down
with feathers from the last
of southward geese,
and in out hearts
where we initial
the passing of each summer,
a memo.

> *Sunshine and Shadow. Birds in the Air.*
> *Star of Bethlehem. Path of Thorns.*
> *North Wind. Lily:*

I have switched
from cloth to jade and crystal,
from the color of gems
to the gems themselves.
Out of the village green
with its rose tree and sheep,
out of the pictographs

48

Catch Me If You Can

of bridge, building, and bird
I have soared
into the heart of green,
the radius of birth
where light begins.
Out of the pages of history
I have swum
to roll in clouds
beyond the reach of alphabet,
beyond the need for words.

> *Road to Tennessee. Chinese Junk.*
> *Church. Frigate. Tide Wheel.*
> *Noon and Night and Winged Square.*
> *Broad Arrow and Courthouse Steps.*
> *Folded Loveletter. Christmas Star:*

Epigraph and epilogue:
What stitch do I use?

Never did Colonial women use
a dragon motif.
I have looked in vain
through centennial squares
but have found no serpent.
There is no burning eye
behind the Tree of Life,
no twisting green in the Pineapple,
no shining scale in the Tulip,
no Yin and Yang in the Nine-Patch,
yet every woman felt--or could have--
what I feel.

Broken Dishes

Storm at Sea. Goose in the Pond.
Drunkard's Path. Save All:

We are connected stitch by stitch,
each day a square,
each year another applique,
this town we celebrate
a tailor's web,
and I have tried to understand.

Still, I stand on my toes,
take off across fences,
houses, historical landmarks,
the hearts that grow from trees.

There is only time to say goodbye.

Ships at Sea. Streak of Lightning.
Baskets or Cake Stand.
Broken Dishes:

No hex can hold me.
No one can see
what is really there.
I have disguised, hidden, covered
what is really there--
and you have, too.
Women, we knew what we were doing.
With each jab of the needle
we knew what we were doing.
All we lack is the hero and the vampire.

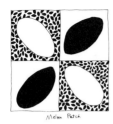
Melon Patch

Chrysanthemum. Magnolia.
Frigate, Lion, and Train.
Weeping Willow Tree:

These threads are like cobwebs
over New England lawns
on August mornings,
like bells from steeples
reaching to bedspreads
keeping us in sleep,
while the train to Bellows Falls
calls along the river tracks.
Connecticut River Valley,
Connecticut River Valley,
where did you go while I traveled?

Peacock. Lover's Knot.
Snake Fence.
Nine-Patch and Bars:

Today, the report
from a friend at Auke Bay
of the single whistling swan
(somewhere, a mate moldering
in snow, in the secret world
of crocuses and rootlight).
We mark our marriage quilt
with hearts and know that hearts
can grow from trees
and quilt our hopes
into our beds.

Birds in the Air #2

Plain, patchwork, and pieced:
We put together the pastoral legend
of our place--a life of cats
with calico eyes and village greens
with tulip trees.

Birds in the Air and
Old Maid's Puzzle.
Tree Everlasting.
Circles. Crosses.
Crosses and Losses.
Rocky Road to Kansas.
Catch Me if You Can:

I could make up diaries
by the hundred, people them
with anecdotes bright
as Amish tulips, serviceable
as laundered cotton quilts,
severe as shipwreck.
I could tell you of another victim
of *Sophia* and the letter she wrote
before she was washed to her death--
of the message she left
for her husband/mother/sister/child/lover
in Topeka/San Francisco/New York.
I could give her a name
and a history
bright as the diamonds
she wore coldly to her death.
I could create this life,
whole cloth.
Because this is an allegory,

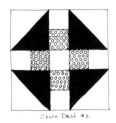
Churn Dash #2

I must give you many
incidents and characters,
but what would I say?

There is only time to say goodbye.

I could write a journal entry
that would break your heart.
What would I say?
"October 25, 1918. Lynn Canal.
The Captain says the *Princess Alice*
will arrive in time,
but there is no time.
Death is on his way,
faster than batteries and steam.
These are the last words
I shall write.
Soon, I shall have no need
for pens and pencils.
I will write myself
in waves along
this angry land.
Where have the years
in the schoolhouse gone?
What have they brought me
but skills I now don't need?
Only the deaf and the blind
will now be able to find my words."

All we lack is the hero and the vampire.

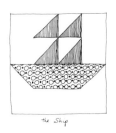

the Ship

I must give you many
incidents and characters,
but what would I say?

And anyone can take a guess.
In 1958, Edison Marshall
published *Princess Sophia*,
"a big, lusty novel of Alaska,"
a terrible book making
ridiculous use of the tragedy.
When he came to Juneau
to collect information,
the man who knew the most
would tell him almost nothing.
According to Marshall,
the passengers, after a
sumptuous last meal,
held a children's party
and sang songs till the end,
drowning without a struggle.
But women and children
were found in life rafts
as far away as Admiralty Island,
and signs of struggle were everywhere.
Death did not come by drowning.

If I were told
I could write one last letter,
to whom would I write?
Li Po (701-762),
bright in the Milky Way.
I would say,
"I do not sing of peach blossoms,

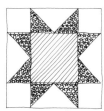
Variable Star #1

bamboo, or sorrowful monkeys
but know the long wind
down from the mountain passes.
Li Po,
little has changed
where winter meets the tree,
and leaf the stream."

And now we seek beyond our galazy
into the Magellanic Clouds,
the next galazies,
tracking for sound
with antennas in Australia,
California, and Spain.

> *Broken Star. Blazing Star.*
> *Falling Star. Travel Star.*
> *Variable Star. Lemon Star.*
> *Star of Bethlehem. Christmas Star.*
> *Feathered Star. Star of Le Moyne.*
> *Cowboy's Star. Star of the West:*

Star of Asses, Birds, and Bones
frozen in lost places,
Star of Babies and Brides,
burn into our hearts,
burn patterns into our hands
that hold the cloth of life.
Help us to see
into the radius of light.

Road to California

I reach out to you, a woman
who has forsaken much--
needle and cloth and picket fence,
diaries and letters home--
a woman who has gone
to live on mountaintops
in cloud and storm,
beyond alphabet,
among amphibians,
where all is wet and green.
I offer you no mementos
but open to you the cloth
of the wild, unbound rain.

> *Kansas Sunflower. Ohio Star.*
> *Flying Swallows.*
> *Cathedral Window:*

While listening to Aaron Copland's
Appalachian Spring, I watch
April seize my neighborhood.
Suddenly I see,
looking across my yard,
the street,
the next yard,
and through the purple bush
blooming against blue clapboard,
and through the window
framed by white shutters,
into the lives of my neighbors,
Thorne and Margit.
(Margit comes from Holland.)
I see them. How can I say this?

56

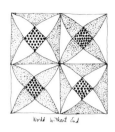
World Without End

I see the light coming out of their heads,
the way there is nothing between them
and the people in the house beyond,
and the house beyond that
all the way across the world,
and that is how we are made.

Arkansas Traveler.
Rainbow. Arrowhead.
Basket of Scraps:

Again, it is April,
a late evening--a farewell party.
Dani is leaving for Mexico
(where the hummingbirds still labor
in geraniums; we cannot change this).
I enter her house on Starr Hill,
where the miners used to live:
dim light in the kitchen
like old gold;
and on the calico cloth, tulips
and a bowl of rye bread, cut thin.
Through the house, I find
more tulips, orange and red,
partly open, and people I know
or do not know.
I walk past tulips,
past zucchini and strawberries
(their seeds worn bravely
on the outside),
and am not afraid to talk
of flying from earth,
my energy ringing behind me

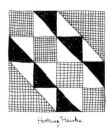
Hovering Hawks

like bells in the minds
of those I have known,
or like a comet,
with its bursting heart.
Joe, Barbara, Marcia, Jan:
Why are we here this night,
tired of politics and corruption,
talking of how we can make it right,
while the tulips keep silent,
keep silent?
And Sarah, who comes from the Aleutians,
bearing a Russian name,
knows everything about
the songs within us,
but she has left early
to go with her daughter
to a movie.

> *Rosette. Cotton Reel.*
> *Missouri Trouble:*

Emily Dickinson said,
"Tell all the Truth but tell it slant--"

> *Hovering Hawks. Hour Glass.*
> *Garden Basket. Windmill:*

I could give you
a quilt of quotations,
picking and choosing as carefully
as Sweet Violet does
among her scraps.
My virtue would be

58

Wild Goose Chase

in tricking you,
in making you think
you had heard a kind of wisdom,
something you could cling to
that would save you from foundering,
something that would make
the script come right.

All we lack is a hero and a vampire.
But the decks are all icy,
and there is only time to say goodbye.

> *Wild Goose Chase.   Wild Goose Chase.*
> *Catch Me if You Can.*

In the center stands the Tree of Life.
On the mountain shakes the spruce
that never felt the sword of thread.

> *Wild Goose Chase.   Wild Goose Chase.*
> *Variable Star.*
> *Broken Star.*
> *Catch Me if You Can.*
> *Catch Me if You Can.*

Former state poet laureate Sheila Nickerson makes her home in Juneau, Alaska's capital city. Her books of poetry include *To the Waters and the Wild*, *Songs of the Pine Wife* and *Waiting for the News of Death*. She is author of the novel, *In Room of Falling Rain*, and of a book of nonfiction, *Writers in the Public Library*.